W9-CYH-359

WITHDRAWN

In My Neighborhood

FIRE FIGHTERS

Paulette Bourgeois

Kim LaFave

KIDS CAN PRESS

Many thanks to the North York Fire Department

P.B. and K.L.

The fire fighters are dozing. But they can hop
out of their beds and into their boots in seconds.

A fire smolders in apartment 804.
"Fire! Fire!" the family screams.
The superintendent calls the fire
department.

The dispatcher gets the
call and alerts the closest
fire station.

The fire fighters slither down the pole or race down the stairs. On go the coats. On go the helmets. On go the boots. There's no confusion. Each fire fighter knows what to do. Only one, two, three minutes have passed since the alarm screeched!

The captain orders the fire fighters to climb the ladders. They break holes in the windows so smoke and fumes can escape.

Other fire fighters attach hoses to hydrants. They spray water onto the flaming building and neighboring buildings so the fire won't spread.

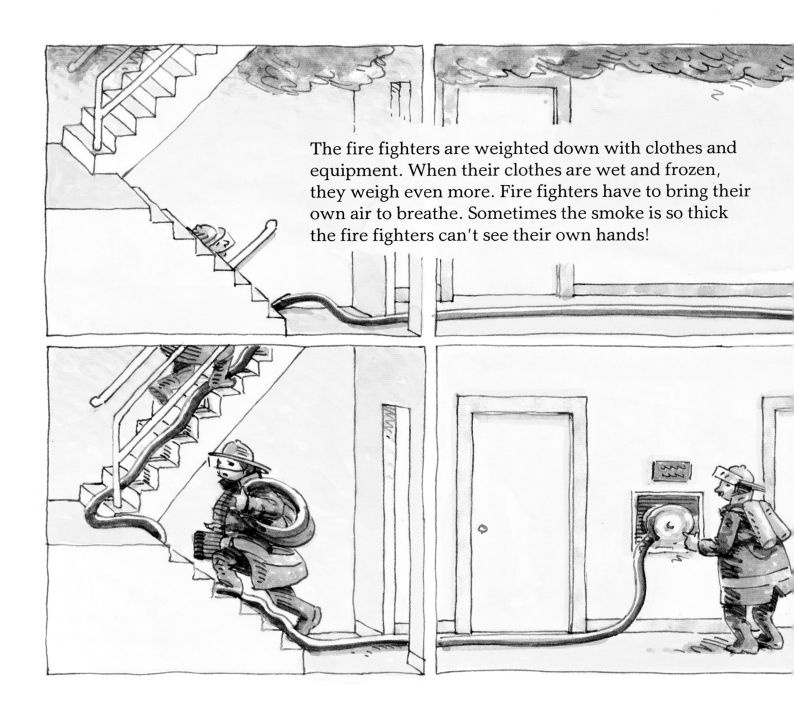

The fire fighters are weighted down with clothes and equipment. When their clothes are wet and frozen, they weigh even more. Fire fighters have to bring their own air to breathe. Sometimes the smoke is so thick the fire fighters can't see their own hands!

Fire fighters usually go to the floor below the burning apartment first. There's no smoke there. They connect their hose and walk up.

The fire fighters climb the stairs and feel their way along the wall. They smash open the door. When they turn on the hose, there's so much water gushing at once that it takes two fire fighters to hold the hose. The water comes out like mist. The fire is so hot that most of the water turns to steam.

Even when the fire is out, the job isn't done. The fire fighters cut off door and window frames to make sure no fire is smoldering behind the woodwork. They clean up most of the mess. But everything is smoky, black and wet.

"Ah, here's the cause of the fire. The plugs are frayed."
Fires leave many clues about how they started. Not everything burns. Sometimes the way the fire burns tells the fire fighters how and where a fire started.

Back at the station, the fire fighters have to clean the truck and equipment. It doesn't matter how tired the fire fighters might be, the work must be done. The equipment has to be ready at all times.

Fire fighters have their own homes and families. But the station is a second home. They sleep there on night shifts. They take turns doing all the chores. They wash the floors, clean the sinks, buy the groceries and cook.

Sometimes it's boring at the station. Fire fighters read, watch television and relax between alarms.

THE PERFECT FIRE FIGHTER

- not too fat, not too thin, not too tall, not too short

- can carry a heavy adult up two sets of stairs

- knows how to fight any kind of fire

- knows how fires start

- knows how to help in an emergency

- can drive a truck quickly and safely

Fire fighters might have to free a trapped passenger from a car. They might have to help sick and injured people.

In the country, volunteers usually fight the fires. They learn how at a special school.

A barn is burning! The farmer calls the fire number. "Beep, beep," screech the pagers. The volunteers drive their own cars to the fire. Some of them go to the regional fire station and get the fire truck.

There are no fire hydrants in the country. The fire fighters bring their own water. And they pump water from ponds, rivers and lakes.

Fire boats protect boats
and the buildings around
harbors. They pump water
straight from the river, lake
or ocean.

Fire boats pump enough water in one minute
to fill a swimming pool. The water shoots out
of water cannons mounted on the deck.

Water bombers dump water on forest fires.

The fire fighters get as close to the fire as they can. They can work for only a few hours at a time because it's so hot. Otherwise they would die from the heat.

They dig trenches to stop the fire from spreading, and they try to smother flames with water or dirt. Sometimes there are no roads to a forest fire. Then fire fighters are parachuted near the fire. They have to walk the rest of the way.

Lightning started this forest fire. Usually careless people start forest fires.

PREVENT FIRES!
Have a family fire safety meeting. Talk about the ways fires can get started. Take a walk around your house or apartment and make sure you follow these rules:

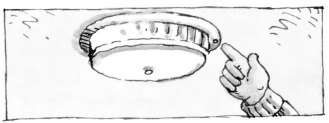

1. There should be smoke detectors on every floor — two on the top floor! Test the smoke detectors every month and keep them clean.

2. Check cords to make sure they are not frayed. Never put wires under rugs or carpets.

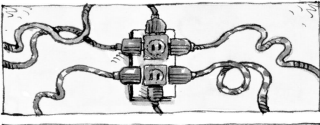

3. Make sure there is only one plug in each receptacle.

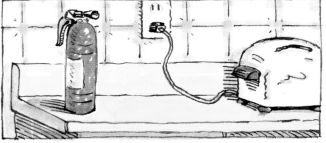

4. Keep a fire extinguisher in the kitchen, in the workroom and in the car. Everyone should know how it is used. Make sure it is always ready to work.

5. Throw out old rags and papers. Keep oily rags in a container with a tight-fitting lid.

6. Never touch anything with this sign. (Flammable)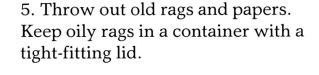

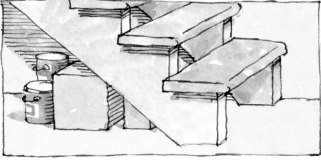

7. Keep the space under stairs clear.

8. Children should never touch matches or lighters. Make sure they are put away in a safe place.

KEEP SAFE

1. Learn to call 911 in case of an emergency. Practice saying your name, address and nearest intersection. Remember that no one should ever call from inside a burning building. Call from a neighbor's home. You can call 911 from a pay phone even if you have no money.

2. Make a family escape plan for your home. Make a drawing of all the rooms in the home. Plan two ways to get out of each room. For some rooms, you may need to buy a hanging ladder to escape out a window. Can you safely climb down the fire escape or jump onto a neighbor's balcony?

3. Practice home fire drills.

4. Decide on a safe place for the family to meet if you must leave your house. Remember that once you get out of a burning building, you must always stay out.

STAY SAFE

If there's smoke or fire:
Yell, "Fire!"

If there is smoke, hold a cloth or towel (wet is best) over your mouth and nose and crawl on the floor to your escape route.

Feel any doors before opening them. If the door is hot — don't open it! Put a blanket or towel (a wet one is best) at the bottom of the door to stop smoke from coming in.

If you cannot open your escape window, throw a chair or other heavy object into the glass to break it. Clear away broken glass before climbing out. Phone the local fire department or dial 911.

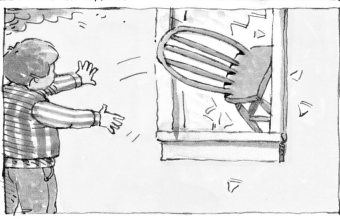

Never, never hide — get out!
Never look for pets or toys — get out!

If your clothes catch fire, never run! Stop! Drop to the ground. Roll on the ground until the flames are out.

There's a fire alarm ringing in your apartment building: Stop everything! Close all windows, then make sure everyone leaves the apartment. Carry your door key in case smoke or fire forces you back inside.

Close the door. Go to a fire exit quickly and calmly.

If your door is hot, stay in your apartment. If you see smoke in the hallway, go back to your apartment. Shut the door and put wet blankets or towels at the base of the door. Open a window and yell "Fire!"

If the fire is in your apartment, yell "Fire!" Get everyone out. Pull the alarm in the hallway. It may not be connected to the fire department. Once you get to a safe place, call 911.

Never use the elevators. Use the fire exit and leave the building. If the escape stairwells are smoky, use the other staircase. If that is blocked, go back to your apartment.

Remember, if you act fire smart, you'll stay fire safe.

First U.S. edition 1998

Text copyright © 1991 by Paulette Bourgeois
Illustrations copyright © 1991 by Kim LaFave

Published in Canada by   Published in the U.S. by
Kids Can Press Ltd.   Kids Can Press Ltd.
29 Birch Avenue   4500 Witmer Industrial Estates
Toronto, ON, M4V 1E2   Niagara Falls, NY 14305-1386

Designed by N.R. Jackson
Typeset by Cybergraphics Co. Inc.
Printed in Hong Kong by Everbest Company Limited

US   98 0 9 8 7 6 5 4 3 2
US PA   00 0 9 8 7 6 5 4 3 2 1

Canadian Cataloguing in Publication Data
Bourgeois, Paulette
    Fire fighters

(In my neighborhood)
ISBN 1-55074-438-0 (bound)   ISBN 1-55074-783-5 (pbk.)

1. Fire fighters — Juvenile literature.   2. Fire extinction —
Juvenile literature.   3. Fire prevention — Juvenile
literature.   I. LaFave, Kim.   II. Title.   III. Series:
Bourgeois, Paulette. In my neighborhood.

TH9148.B69 2000   j363.37   C97-931104-7

Kids Can Press is a Nelvana company